ACADEMIC CHANGE AND THE LIBRARY FUNCTION

Papers Delivered at
a Meeting of the College
and Research Division
Pennsylvania Library Association
October 1969

C. WALTER STONE
Compiler

PENNSYLVANIA LIBRARY ASSOCIATION
1970

Library of Congress Catalog Card No. 71-120169
Copyright Pennsylvania Library Association 1970

Room 506, 200 South Craig Street
Pittsburgh, Pennsylvania 15213

CONTENTS

Dr. Stone has been director of the University of Pittsburgh Libraries since 1965. Immediately prior to assuming that position, he was professor in the Graduate School of Library and Information Sciences at the University of Pittsburgh. Dr. Stone served with the U.S. Office of Education for several years, directing its educational media branch from 1960-1962. From 1949-1960, he was professor of library science at the University of Illinois. Long concerned with the world of educational media and well attuned to the environment of change, Dr. Stone was notably qualified to moderate the meeting for which the following papers were prepared.

INTRODUCTION

The three papers which follow this introduction were first presented at a meeting held in Pittsburgh on October 3, 1969, by the College and Research Division of the Pennsylvania Library Association. Their purpose was to review for consideration of those concerned with higher education in the Commonwealth the changing character and responsibilities of the American college and university, the changing methods and media required for improvement of academic instruction, and the implications which both of these hold for the future optimum development of college and university library and information services.

The author of each paper has distilled in relatively brief compass knowledge and individual points of view garnered from many years of national and international concern as a specialist working with the problems, issues, and ideas set forth. The logic of sequence observed in this publication, as in the original conference session, led Dr. Tyler to present first a picture of the changing scene in American higher education viewed from forty-seven years of active involvement as a professor, administrator, and educational consultant. Dr. Brown's approach, augmented in the platform version by use of a two-screen slide presentation, calls upon college and university librarians to acknowledge and at last to act upon an understanding of the fact that library functions must change radically, that libraries must become multipurpose agencies, and that librarians must be more intimately concerned with how information is found, manipulated, assessed, and used to achieve instructional purposes as well as to provide repositories. Professor Kent sees the future performance of the library functions consistent with the changing objectives and methodology of both research and teaching in higher education as requiring a technological revolution in which the capabilities of modern computer technology are harnessed to the full, both for purposes of information transfer and control as well as for data storage. And, in part, because of the economics of the situation, he predicts an expansion of college and university library service to include direct and aggressive marketing of that portion of recorded knowledge-access actually capable of sale and for which suitable cost recovery programs may be established (thus enabling sponsoring institutions to augment their resources by sharing costs with noncampus groups).

Although each paper was drafted independently with knowledge only of the main theme of the others to be prepared, there are several points of unity which might be regarded as an underlying theme. For example, each stresses the changes taking place in higher education which call for an ever more individualized approach to a broadening range of instructional and research resources. Each directly, or by implication, stresses library responsibility to attain greater relevance to user requirements and, indeed, to feature the *user* as a primary focus of concern in educational and library planning and development. Tyler's paper stresses the future importance of junior colleges; the need for more separation of research and graduate instruction from undergraduate activities; an increasing importance of small institutions (enrolling less than 2,000 students) despite apparent trends to the contrary; changes in college grading systems; growing emphasis on work-study programs; and the mounting interest and concern with which higher education will be regarded by students, parents, and employers (as well as the increased attention which the college and university must give larger numbers coming from more limited, i.e., working class, socio-economic backgrounds) — all providing major challenges which must be directly reflected in plans concerned with the utility of what is taught or learned. Brown highlights the need for a general "dressing-up" of the whole business of college teaching. And Kent extends a plea for the use of modern techniques and technology to "satisfy the need for access to recorded knowledge by providing rapidly, conveniently, economically, and with precision, that portion of the current and previous literature that will be useful:

—to a particular individual,
—at a particular time,
—for a particular problem or interest,
—and in a form that is useful to him,

CHANGING
RESPONSIBILITIES
OF HIGHER
EDUCATION

RALPH W. TYLER

Dr. Ralph W. Tyler, former director of the Center for Advanced Study in the Behavioral Sciences, Stanford, California, has been involved in education since he began his career almost fifty years ago as a high-school teacher. An alumnus of Doane College, Dr. Tyler earned his Ph.D. at the University of Chicago. His positions at the University of Nebraska, University of North Carolina, Ohio State University, and University of Chicago led in 1948 to his assumption of the deanship of Chicago's Division of Social Sciences. He served as dean until 1953. That year he left Chicago in order to play a principal role in the establishment of the Center for Advanced Study in the Behavioral Sciences. Dr. Tyler was its director until 1967. Since leaving the directorship, Dr. Tyler has served as consultant, lecturer, and visiting scholar. He is also a director of Science Research Associates.

Dr. Tyler's advisory positions include service to many organizations. Among them are the National Science Board, the Research and Development Panel of the U.S. Office of Education, the National Advisory Council on Disadvantaged Children, and the National Academy of Education. He is also an active member of the Social Science Research Council, the Armed Forces Institute, the National Society for the Study of Education, the American Association for the Advancement of Science, the American Statistical Association, the National Education Association, and the American Educational Research Association.

CHANGING RESPONSIBILITIES
OF HIGHER EDUCATION

INTRODUCTION

An audience of professional librarians does not need to be reminded of the tremendous changes under way in colleges and universities as well as in all levels of education. The applications of science and technology to agriculture, industry, business, defense, and the health services have not only sharply increased per capita production and shifted the balance of the economy in the direction of the production of nonmaterial services, but they have also greatly modified the composition of the labor force and markedly increased the demand for educated persons. A century ago, more than eighty per cent of the American labor force was engaged in producing and distributing material goods. The means of production leaned heavily on unskilled and semi-skilled workers who comprised three-fourths of the labor force. More than half was engaged in agriculture.

Today, the production and distribution of material goods requires only forty per cent of the labor force while sixty per cent is employed in furnishing nonmaterial services: education, health services, recreation, social services, science, engineering, accounting, and administration. Less than seven per cent is engaged in agriculture; less than five per cent is unskilled. Only a few Americans without education can obtain employment. To qualify beyond the level of the unskilled requires roughly the equivalent of a fifth-grade education. Yet, heretofore, no nation has been able to reach and to educate all its children. In the United States today and in other western nations, somewhere between fifteen per cent and twenty-five per cent of the children do not gain the equivalent of a fifth-grade education. Our elementary schools are facing a very important new task — to reach every child and to enable him to gain an elementary education.

Secondary schools are also confronting new tasks. The new jobs developing in our technological society are in occupations that depend heavily on intellectual and social skills as in health services, education, social services, engineering, science, accounting, and administration. Heretofore, most youth whose aspirations led to these occupations were either girls or boys from homes in which one or more parents were in these occupations. Boys from working-class homes generally aspired to jobs requiring physical strength or manual dexterity. Now, the demand for personnel for these new jobs is far greater than can be supplied by youth who come from middle-class backgrounds. To reach youth from working-class homes and to enable them to gain intellectual and social skills is a new task for the American high school.

BACKGROUND

The profound transformations of our society are similarly creating new tasks for American colleges and universities. Looking backward in time, we find that most changes that have taken place in American institutions of higher education have been responses to changes in the larger society and can be understood more adequately against this background. Until the Second World War, the effects of science and technology on the economy and particularly on the composition of the labor force were in limited sectors and resulted in gradual adjustments. The colonial colleges and universities made few modifications of the institutions adapted from England that prepared their students for the occupational, social, and political élite. The students were drawn largely from the upper-middle and upper-classes of American society, although a few young men from lower social and educational backgrounds were able to gain enrollment and help to provide a certain degree of social mobility in the society. As the country began to develop industry, commercial farming, and transportation systems, a demand was created for a marked increase in the numbers of those prepared for leadership and technical roles in these fields and for the service professions that grew with industrial expansion, namely law and medicine. The existing colleges were largely unresponsive to the requests from the growing agricultural and mechanical classes to enroll their children and to give attention to the substance of their needs. The common reply to these pressures was, "Your young people are not college material. They don't even have a command of Latin and Greek. Furthermore, science, engineering and agriculture are vocational subjects unfit for college study."

The upshot of this conflict was the passage by the Congress in 1862 of the Morrill Act, which offered Federal land to every state that would establish a college "to serve the agriculture and mechanical classes." Thus the Land Grant Colleges were founded, not through internal reform but by the use of Federal inducements.

The changes in American higher education represented by the founding and development of the Land Grant Colleges arose from the growth of commercial farming, industry, and business during the nineteenth century with corresponding new educational demands and increasing numbers and influence of commercial farmers and businessmen. Changes now taking place are in large measure responses of higher education to new societal needs and new political and social forces. Earlier, I cited the great transformation taking place in the American economy. The United States is the first nation to have developed technology to a point where less than half of its labor force (only forty per cent in 1967) is required to furnish material goods, thus freeing a majority of its members to meet the demands for health, education, recreation, welfare, and knowledge.

These changes in the larger society have been reflected in the increased enrollments in colleges and universities. At the turn of the century, three per cent of the age group entered college; now it is forty per cent. This tremendous expansion is due to the interaction of several factors, namely, the labor force demand for college graduates, the rising aspirations of the American people as they see the opportunities available for them and their children which are contingent upon college education, and the response of public and private sources for greatly enlarged support. But these demands and the increased enrollments confront colleges and universities with new responsibilities.

New Tasks

If American higher education is to be responsive to the developing needs, it must learn how to attract, stimulate and aid the learning of youth coming from families in which no one has previously attended college. A majority of these young people are skeptical regarding the value of abstract knowledge and their aspirations have not included the development of intellectual and social skills. They have little confidence that they can learn much from lectures and books. They have had previously few intimate contacts with persons engaged in intellectual activity who could serve as live models for their own guidance.

A second new task is the review and rebuilding of curricula in colleges and universities based on the premise that the subject-matter disciplines are not ends in themselves but are resources to aid individual students and the wider community in dealing with their problems and in living in ways that give life greater meaning, greater effectiveness, and greater satisfactions. The current, oft-repeated complaint that the college curriculum is irrelevant to today's problems indicates that colleges have not helped students to see that the problems of great concern to them such as war and peace, environmental pollution, race relations, continuing poverty, and lack of respect and recognition for the individual, can be understood more freely and attacked more effectively on the basis of knowledge, insights, and skills that are furnished by scholarly disciplines. Contemporary scholarship does not provide answers to these critical problems nor does it substitute for interest, concern, dedication, energy, and courage in attacking them. Today's problems, however, will not be solved simply through intense involvement. There are no instant solutions. Successful treatment of them requires planning, systematic attention to all the major facets, and comprehensive coordinated efforts of many individuals and groups. The development of more adequate understanding, the design of approaches to the problem, and the planning of effective coordinated operations can be enlightened by the various disciplines if the relevant contributions they can make are identified and worked into forms that enable students to gain the understanding and the skills required. Most college curricula have developed as accretions from the continuing work of scholars, and the potential contributions have not been rigorously reviewed, selected, and organized in terms of their value to students and to contemporary society.

In the rebuilding of curricula, certain new objectives will need to be given emphasis. Each course should furnish a clear demonstration of what kinds of problems and content the discipline deals with, how it simplifies complex reality in order to make study manageable, the way in which study is carried on, the basic concepts it uses in order to organize and interpret the phenomena studied, the kinds of facts and generalizations obtained from study, and how this kind of study throws light on significant areas of human concern. This demonstration is needed to help the student understand and appreciate what the discipline has to offer. Each course should also furnish continuing opportunity for the student to carry on study in this discipline that relates directly to matters which he considers important.

Emphasis also needs to be given to helping the student learn how to learn. The so-called knowledge explosion reminds us that scholarship is not static. A student cannot expect during his college career to acquire all the important facts and generalizations that will be helpful to him in the years ahead. Jerome Wiesner, President Kennedy's science advisor, estimated that scientific knowledge is doubling every ten or fifteen years. In this case, the amount of new knowledge available ten or fifteen years after graduation will be as great as the knowledge that existed when one is in college. In order to utilize adequately the growing resources of scholarship the modern student needs to find how to continue his learning throughout his active life. Hence, in college, he needs to learn how to use resources that he can tap when teachers, lecturers and other formal educational devices are not available, and to develop the habit of doing so.

For students to become life-long learners, drawing upon scholarship in attacking critical problems, the colleges and universities must become centers of "problem-solving" in which students are engaged as junior colleagues with others who are working seriously on these problems. Not only will the faculty be involving students in their own problem-solving work, but arrangements will need to be developed with many other public and private agencies that are working on relevant problems. Some agencies at the local, state, and national levels furnish appropriate settings for students to be involved in working on such problems as health, housing, traffic congestion, crime, child-rearing, education, new technologies, and the intellectual problems of the various sciences. The arts and humanities are not so commonly recognized as fields in which students may be junior partners with mature artists, writers, dramatists, and the like, but these disciplines can illuminate life choices and afford bases for understanding wider potentials for a meaningful and satisfying life.

Heretofore, colleges and universities have been wary about establishing working relations with other agencies of the community because they feared that the unique contribution of the educational institution would be lost. There is always the danger that close association will erase the significant differences among the associates, but this danger can be reduced or eliminated if each of the associates is clear about his role. The university's role is to provide a "knowledge-base" for study and action and to help students use the concepts, skills, and insights which the disciplines furnish as they work in these agencies. Through classes, seminars, libraries and laboratories, conversations, observations, and other means that universities can devise, students are aided in drawing upon the resources of scholarship in understanding what goes on in the cooperating agencies and in working out their own roles and jobs more intelligently.

Because both scholarship and critical problems are not restricted within national boundaries, American higher education is becoming internationally minded. The participation of American colleges and universities in international programs is already widespread, but we lack widely-accepted policies and plans for determining the nature and extent of participation on the part of an individual institution. However, it is clear that leaders in politics, business, and agriculture are increasingly examining critical problems in world perspective rather than only from a local or national point of view. It is also clear that many of these world problems cannot be attacked effectively without the cooperative contributions of well-informed and well-educated people throughout the world. Neither the United States nor the western community of nations can adequately cope with worldwide problems. These facts indicate that faculties and students will be increasingly involved in seeking a more international perspective for their work on problems and in participating in international or cross-national projects. Scholarly collections of books and reports, maps, pictures, and other sources of facts, and informed opinions relevant to world interests and world perspectives will need to be built in order to support the instructional and research programs of educational institutions and of action agencies. Programs for educating foreign students in America and American students abroad will be given more critical review to insure an efficient use of these more costly arrangements — efficient in the sense that they represent an economical means for students to acquire world perspective and ability to cooperate with those from other nations in work on world problems. From the standpoint of the faculty member, international aspects of his work will be increasingly considered, but the extent to which this involves him in extensive work abroad will depend on similar economic judgments. How far will his scholarly work be enhanced by study and was in equilibrium with salaries somewhat lower than those paid to persons with similar levels of education outside academia. The division of responsibility for policy-making among trustees, administrators, and faculty members typically gave the faculty major responsibility for curriculum and instruction, and partial responsibility for admissions policies, student affairs, and discipline. In most institutions, decisions regarding establishment of programs, new schools, salaries, and teaching-loads were made by the trustees on recommendation of the president.

Since 1947, the great increase in numbers of students and in funds for research has created unprecedented demand for faculty members. The equilibrium has shifted. In general, salaries are higher, teaching-loads are lighter, faculty members have assumed major responsibility for policies regarding research and teaching, and have much greater influence than earlier on the establishment of new programs and schools, and the conduct of students. But this situation will change. The unprecedented numbers of students in graduate schools are beginning to swell the ranks of prospective faculty members. In ten years, the equilibrium of supply and demand for college faculty will result in a relatively lower salary position than at present.

A second factor that is changing the equilibrium of control in higher institutions is the pressure of student protests. At least three types of student activists are now identified. There are the "Black Organizations" and other minority groups who press for more of the educational advantages that have been obtained by the visible majority. At present they are unclear about the steps required to get a good education, but they know that present college programs in general are not giving them the advantages thought to derive from college experience. They are being failed out in large percentages, which fact they blame on having to take hard courses and being graded by an unfair marking system. So they ask for "Black Departments," and largely elective curricula. They will discover after a while that the root of their problems is an educational system and a faculty not designed for students who come from backgrounds of limited education. Then they will press for the faculty to give major attention to their education and learning.

A second protest group of students are those who come largely from middle-class backgrounds and who want to be involved in learning that is relevant to their own plans and aspirations. They seek

education that gives them new and grander visions, new and more
fundamental understanding, and intellectual and social skills with
which they can deal with life and the world. Instead, they find un-
inspired courses that seem to have no connection with life as they
know it and as they hope it will be. They find teachers who seem unable
to communicate with them and apparently uninterested in them. They
seek wholesale educational reform. This pressure, as it builds up, is
certain to influence faculty members in their attention to the curriculum, teaching, and learning.

A third type of protest group consists of those who belong to or
support the organization called "Students for a Democratic Society."
They believe that contemporary American society is so hypocritical,
so corrupt, so engrossed in material production and in maintaining
and conforming to rigid institutions that there is no hope for its reform.
They are the present-day anarchists whose professed goal is to destroy
colleges and universities in the hope that they can take leadership in
rebuilding higher education. Their influence is likely to confuse
pressures for genuine reform and to give some support to those who
want no change. However, the present trends seem to indicate clearly
that students will be heard and will have a significant influence on
policy-making both through policy committees of faculty and administration on which they will be represented, and through articulation
in public and private of their views. Their influence will bring about an
increase in the effectiveness of colleges and universities.

Parents of the new groups of students now enrolled in higher
education are becoming another pressure group that will, for a time,
increasingly influence policy-making in colleges and universities. A
recent Gallup poll shows that ninety-seven per cent of the parents
interviewed want their children to enter college. Parents who have
not attended college view higher education as a major means to insure
a bright future for their children. Hence, many of them are deeply
concerned with the success of their sons and daughters in going
through college and getting the appropriate credentials. Reports that
are brought home about the neglect and indifference of the professors
arouse parents to protest and to seek means of influencing the college.
They are not likely to have a massive effect from direct confrontation
with the faculty or administration of the college, but they are likely to
cultivate two lines of influence. One is through the legislature in case
their child is in a state college or university, and the other is through

their effort to select a college that is reported to give "poor boys" a square deal. The latter force will be greatly accentuated if the proposal from the Carnegie Commission on Higher Education is adopted, which would provide funds for the student to use at the college or university of his choice. At present, the nearly monopolistic position of state colleges and universities re-enforces the majority faculty ideology, since there is no great competition among colleges with different views about education. Whatever means become available, parents of students from lower income levels will increasingly be heard because they perceive education as the major means of advancement for their children. For the middle classes, education is less critical since the parents have access to a wider range of occupational opportunities. This explains why parents in the past have not played so large a role in college policy-making.

The major employers of college graduates will continue to exercise a significant influence on policies in institutions of higher education through trustees, legislators, and financial grants. Programs in engineering, business, and nursing have frequently been adopted by colleges and universities due to the pressures of groups who employ graduates in these areas. When graduates in one of these fields are in short supply, representatives from employers' groups have found it helpful to their interests to contact the college administration which then selected faculty members to devise new programs, to recruit new types of students, to adopt new qualifying standards, and the like. This process is likely to be accentuated in the future because of the rising demands in the service occupations that can be met only by recruiting from a much wider range of youth than has heretofore been enrolled. The new enrollees will require more attention by the faculty to the curriculum and to teaching and learning, if the students are to be successful. The college will be judged by the employers in terms of its success in providing competent persons in these fields. For this reason, the influence of employer groups places emphasis upon effective education.

For the past ten years, some industries and chambers of commerce have sought to increase the amount of research conducted in the sciences in their regions because they believed that the concentrating of scientific research activities attracted new industries. Recent experience does not support this belief, nor is it possible to raise the level of research activity substantially in a large number of places. Actually, the concentration of technical industries in such areas as Boston, the Bay Region of California, Los Angeles, and Rochester, New York, is much less attributable to the research activities of the neighboring universities than it is to the availability of technically-trained personnel — an effective educational system is more essential than a concentration of research activities. As this is becoming understood, the pressure for general increases in the research activities of colleges and universities will not be continued by industrial and civic organizations in the region.

A major influence that will affect the structure and functioning of institutions of higher education during the next two decades is the allocation of financial resources. Not only will the amount of funds made available be critical, but their differential distribution to different institutions for different purposes and the conditions under which they are granted will have far-reaching consequences. At the present time, the money allocated to a publicly-controlled college or university has been largely based on the number of students enrolled. Little or no attempt has been made to question the principle that increasing numbers of students require corresponding increases in annual operating funds. The support of research by the states has been obtained largely through internal allocations by the university of funds furnished on the basis of student enrollment. Research support by the Federal government has been based primarily on the number and quality of proposals submitted to the funding agency and not on the basis of the effect on the college or the relevance of the research undertaken to the educational mission of the institution. In the privately-controlled colleges and universities, funds are allocated to a major extent through a market mechanism in which students choose the institution and pay the fees, and donors choose the institution and pay for things that they value in the college. The larger private universities also obtain research funds from Federal agencies on the same basis as public institutions.

This method of allocating resources is changing. The continuing increase in enrollments, the rising costs of operation, and the increasing criticism of effectiveness are stimulating re-examination of the system of allocation. Unquestioning acceptance of traditional policies and practices is disappearing, and colleges and universities are being asked to justify requests by rough cost-benefit analysis of alternative proposals. This is revealing the confusion that arises from mixing research costs with teaching costs, from treating credit-hours of instruction as though it were an output rather than a particular way of arranging instruction, from failing to assess what students have learned, and what contribution each research enterprise has made. In short, the increasing demand for rational bases to justify resource allocation is likely to have powerful influence on the folklore of academic life, placing value on effectiveness and efficiency rather than on conspicuous expenditure.

THE EMERGING PATTERNS

It is important to recognize that the patterns of higher education in this country will continue to be in flux since our society is a dynamic, changing one. An effort to describe probable characteristics of colleges and universities in the next two decades is based on a projection of present active forces, several of which are in conflict, and to focus attention at a point ten years hence, when the changes now under way or incipient will have reached a further stage of evolution. What is predicted in the following section is based on an assessment of the outcome, ten years hence, of present movements. It is likely to err both in the estimates of the strength and of the rate of movement of present forces, and in being unaware of new forces that may become involved in higher education that are not now on the scene.

The characteristic which seems most clearly to be predictable for the future is the increase in the importance of the community and junior colleges. They now enroll more than twenty per cent of all students in post-high-school institutions, and at the rate these colleges are increasing in number as well as in enrollment, it is safe to predict that ten years from now three million students will be enrolled in community and junior colleges, representing one-third of the total post-high-school enrollment and approximately one-half of all first- and second-year students. Their importance is due to several factors. They are generally open-door colleges, enrolling nearly all high-school graduates or adults who apply. Because the students represent a very wide range of background and previous educational experience, the faculty generally recognizes the need for students to be helped to learn. Hence, more attention is given in these colleges to the curriculum, the relevance of courses, the appropriateness of the textbooks and other reading materials, and the use of audio-visual aids. These institutions are recognized as serving the community in which they exist

so that students, parents, employers, and other leading citizens are able
to present their points of view and interests to which the college seeks
to respond. They also differ from the traditional four-year colleges
in permitting wide variations in attendance patterns, including night
classes, alternation of work and study by terms or even years, and
part-time attendance while the student is employed in a full- or part-
time job, or is largely occupied with home responsibilities. Because
these colleges generally recognize that they have special responsibilities
that differ from those assumed by the traditional four-year colleges,
the faculty is recruited in large numbers from high-school teachers and
persons with experience in industry, agriculture, and service occupations. Hence, they are more in tune with student and community
expectations. Furthermore, the per capita cost of education is usually
much lower in the junior and community colleges than in other institutions of higher education.

The only forces now observable that might operate to reduce the
growing importance of junior and community colleges are the attrac-
tion of the faculty to the conditions thought to prevail in the traditional
four-year colleges and the prestige which some community members
believe is attached to the presence of a four-year college in that community. Typically, teaching loads are lighter in four-year colleges,
and the faculty members assume less responsibility for constructive
contacts with students. From the vantge point of the junior college, a
professor in a four-year college does little work and is free to write,
to think, to lecture, and to play. From a somewhat similar viewpoint,
some community leaders see the establishment of a four-year college
in their community as a symbol of status, having moved "beyond"
preoccupation with the education of students for constructive lives in
the community to education for élite positions and for leisure. These
two forces produce a similar interest in changing the junior or community college into a four-year college or university. It appears un-
likely that this interest will gain sufficient support to affect the present
strong trend toward increased importance for the junior or community college.

A second feature that seems likely to emerge within ten years is
the increased separation between the structures and functions assigned
to undergraduate education, particularly the education of freshmen
and sophomores, and those to research and graduate education. At
present, colleges and universities oppose this separation because cur-

rent operations depend heavily upon reciprocal relations between upper and lower divisions. In large universities, graduate students gain major support from serving as teaching assistants in undergraduate courses. Commonly, funds are obtained on the basis of total enrollment in which undergraduates, even freshmen and sophomores, yield amounts of support in excess of that spent on them, while research and graduate instruction consume the excess provided from the undergraduate allotments. Furthermore, large undergraduate enrollments justify large departments, which can thus support greater specialization of faculty members and a certain number of "stars," who bring prestige to the institution. Finally, some institutions believe that large undergraduate enrollments are likely to support strong athletic programs.

The forces that seem likely to bring about greater separation of research and graduate instruction from undergraduate education include students and parents and demands from funding agencies for accounting by function and for greater efficiency. Student and parent pressures are strongly directed to the neglect of students by senior faculty members. The use of student assistants and the infrequent contact with "real professors" are two points that appear again and again in student complaints. When faculty members try to meet these protests by giving serious attention to the education of students, they find little time for research. Hence, those who view themselves primarily as scholars and scientists rather than as teachers are unhappy with the changed situation. Some accept offers to go to another institution which promises more time for research. Others want to be appointed as "research professors" or to become members of research institutes which have no undergraduate teaching function. Some point to the system in the Soviet Union as a desirable example. In Russia, research institutes are separate from the universities, thus clearly defining professional responsibilities.

Funding agencies are pressing for better accounting and more efficient university operations. Legislatures find it difficult to understand why the state university reports a per capita annual cost of the education of undergraduates as two to five times that of junior colleges, when the investigations of later academic achievement show that junior college students of similar scholastic aptitude-rating do as well in upper division work as do students who were in the university during their freshman and sophomore years. The apparent inefficiency of the university in its conduct of undergraduate education may not be wholly a matter of inappropriate accounting procedures. It is also probable that faculty members who are rewarded for their research and writing but at the same time are responsible for undergraduate courses are less likely to give thought and time to their undergraduate students than are junior college teachers whose chief responsibility is teaching.

A clearer separation not only would increase the likelihood that the faculty assigned to undergraduate education would give more attention to learning, teaching, and the curriculum, but that it would furnish a basis for a more objective and ethical assessment of research productivity. The folklore that every teacher should also be a researcher had a good influence, when it was promulgated at the end of World War I, in developing research interests and attitudes favorable to research in an otherwise pragmatic society. But as a means of training people for research or furnishing an efficient basis for obtaining new knowledge it has been grossly inefficient. Most persons when they receive the degree of Ph.D. require experience on the job to become effective researchers. This is not surprising. In medicine, law, engineering, and business administration, for example, university education provides only one component of preparation for the professions. Experience on the job, preferably with skilled guidance, is necessary for the development of a competent professional. In similar fashion, every graduate student preparing for research will need research experience under skilled guidance, but this does not mean that every professor in graduate school needs to have his own research laboratory. Research institutes under university control, research laboratories and centers operated by public agencies or by private firms or nonprofit organizations, could serve as on-the-job training institutions. When funding agencies require objective, critical appraisal of a university's research program in terms of the efficiency of its research production and its training of research personnel, many readjustments are likely to be made that separate more clearly the responsibilities of undergraduate education from research and research training.

Even when it is recognized that the research enterprise can be more efficiently conducted when it is not confused with undergraduate education, concern will be expressed over the danger that the undergraduate teacher will be obsolete and no longer abreast of scholarship unless he is actively engaged in research. Disregarding the fact that evidence has not been obtained to indicate that those undergraduate

Because of the concern of students for the relevance of education to their own interests, problems, and plans, much more use will be made of direct experience in learning and less dependence on lectures and reading. Cooperative education — the planned correlation between work experience and education on the campus — will be greatly expanded. During the past five years, the number of colleges employing cooperative education has more than doubled. This form of education helps to relate the student to the world of work, gives him a sense of confidence in his adult potential, helps to give meaning to what he is learning in college, and furnishes income to defray some of his expenses. Expanded to public and voluntary agencies, it becomes a major laboratory for college education.

The wide range of student abilities, interests, and backgrounds will stimulate the establishment of a variety of admission policies among the many colleges and universities in this country. Most of the junior and community colleges will continue to admit any youth who has graduated from high school and any adult who presents evidence of interest and basic background required for the course he intends to pursue. Some institutions will restrict their admissions to applicants who have made high grades in high school and high scores on scholastic aptitude tests. Others will select in ways designed to achieve a "student mix" — a composition believed to be favorable to active learning which is commonly defined as including students from various races and ethnic backgrounds, with a variety of interests and achievements in school, extracurricular, and community activities. Still others will select students in terms of occupational interests or other bases for specialization in college and university. Some states will follow the California pattern which specifies the kinds of students that are admissible to each of the three systems of public higher education in that state. In general, every high-school graduate who wants to go to college will be admissible to some institution within one hundred miles of his residence.

Staffing patterns will be modified by the needs created by the changes in curricula, in teaching and learning practices, and in the relationship to the research and graduate institutions. The ratio of students to teachers in the institution will be higher than the present average of four-year institutions but probably not as high as the average student-teacher ratio in junior colleges. The use of such technological devices as overhead projectors, motion pictures, video tapes, closed-circuit TV, audio recorders, and computers will increase as students discover their values in the learning process. The addition of these devices will not be the occasion for reducing the number of faculty members, but rather for increasing the effectiveness of learning.

Mention has been made earlier of the shift in forces exerting influences and partial control on colleges and universities. It seems probable that students and their parents will have more influence than at present through representation on internal committees, through membership on advisory boards, through membership on boards of trustees, through direct confrontation with faculty members and administrators, and through lawmakers. Potential employers will have more influence because more of them now seek college-trained personnel. Their influence will be exerted through financial grants, through direct persuasion with faculty members and administrators, through boards of trustees, and through lawmakers. Legislators will have more influence because the need for public funds has grown more acute and legislators are demanding reviews by the university of its policies, programs, and practices. This applies primarily to state legislators; however, the Congress will also exert a powerful influence.

At present, faculty members have the greatest influence of all groups on university policy; the influence of administrators is lower than in the past. Ten years from now, as these other forces exert strong efforts, the faculty power will be reduced and the administrators' influence will rise because the administration is in a better position to deal constructively with external forces than is the faculty.

Conclusion

The foregoing essay presents a picture of the changing scene in American higher education as I view it from forty-seven years of active involvement as a professor, administrator, and consultant. Great changes are now going on in colleges and universities. They face new tasks, they find that they are involved with students who differ in significant respects from those they have known before. They are encountering new pressures from new sources — student protests, faculty unrest, research demands, parent displeasure, and increasing financial problems. In this flux of difficulties, all colleges and universities will not respond in the same way, but I believe that some of the directions of movement can be foreseen and I have reported them here. Only time can prove the validity or error of these projections.

This effort to recognize the essential differences and yet coordinate purposes of *informing* and *teaching* has led some in higher education toward the so-called "systems approach." This term itself is difficult to define. However, one fairly useful definition is that it is the materials, equipment, and other interrelated elements (including human components) of an assemblage that operate in an organized manner in handling the appropriate encoding of instructional messages and the distribution, manipulation, use, and refinement of information. To be effective, such a system must be sensitive to various stimuli and include elements for appropriate response, feedback, and adjustment.

In the remainder of this paper I will explore more fully the several elements and procedures involved in developing an instructional system for an institution of higher education.

What, then, are the necessary elements of the system? In its simplest form, the development of an instructional system for the curriculum of an institution of higher learning requires attention to a number of processes which, for present convenience, may be grouped under six headings: (1) instructional purposes and goals, (2) the status, capabilities, and goals of students, as participants in the system, (3) the status and capabilities of professors and corollary professionals and technical staff associated with its teaching-learning activities, (4) the status and capabilities of certain nonhuman resources of the institution, (5) ways of implementing and managing the logistics of the system, and (6) program evaluation and improvement.

First in importance for the instructional system, and probably the most difficult of all to develop, is the need for clear definition of the purposes and goals of instruction — the educational objectives. Educational objectives have been defined by Benjamin Bloom in *Taxonomy of Educational Objectives* (pages 26-27) as:

> ... explicit formulations of the ways in which students are expected to be changed by the educative process. That is, the ways, in which they will change in their thinking, their feelings, and their actions. . . . The formulation of educational objectives is a matter of conscious choice on the part of the teaching staff. . . . It should be clear . . . that objectives are not only the goals toward which the curriculum is shaped and toward which instruction is guided, but they are also the goals that provide the detailed specification for the construction and use of evaluative techniques.

With respect to the students, the questions must be asked: Do they understand and do they accept as valid and significant the objectives which have been developed? What has been their role in developing them?

We all know professors whose concepts of "goals" or "objectives" revolve mainly around covering (or "uncovering") the subject largely through linear, one-way, logical, step-by-step explication. We know, too, how difficult it is, and how difficult it is likely to continue to be to change this approach, to move toward the development and statement of objectives that are clear and precise with respect to what is to be accomplished in the course or program, what the student who finishes it will know, what he will be able to do, how he will feel or think, and at what level of proficiency. But such statements are necessary if we are to know what it is expected the instructional system ought to *do* — how it will affect (and, hopefully, change and improve) those who experience it.

Second in the process of developing a systematic instructional program, attention must be directed toward students who participate in it. Data must be gathered to show where they stand initially with respect to the specific instructional goals just described. Discovery and use of such information are necessary if students are to be freed from lock-step, uniform instruction, if they are to be given opportunities to tune in or out of a system according to their individual capabilities or requirements.

Efforts must also be made to identify other special characteristics of students influencing choices within the system. Who among them, for example, has a record of past experience, training, or skill-development which may be capitalized upon in the program? Who seems most capable of proceeding more or less independently in their studies? Who will profit most from "large-group," "regular-group," or "one-to-one" instruction?

A third consideration of the system described here is the status of professors and of corollary professionals and technical staff involved. Perhaps a team approach involving insightful combinations of large-group, medium-group, small-group, and independent activities will be employed. Who is suggested as the logical "manager"? Who among the staff promises best performance as large-group lecturer, as television demonstrator, as small-group discussion leader, as laboratory supervisor, as editorial contributor to course syllabi, as evaluation expert, or as liaison representative with the library or educational media center? What are the capabilities of necessary back-up personnel — media production specialists, equipment operators, computer operators and programmers? What staff capabilities must be developed from scratch, or at least improved, before the process will succeed?

A fourth consideration of the instructional system involves the status and capabilities of essential nonhuman resources of the "mother" system — the institution itself. Such questions as these must be answered: Are the print collections and the audio-visual collections of the institution sufficiently rich, and suitably administered and controlled, to contribute effectively to the achievement of program objectives? Which functions related to those objectives may be performed adequately (or best, or most economically) by: (a) *instruments alone* —mechanical, electronic, electrical—in some of which materials (films, cassette tape recordings, video tapes, slides, or others) are used, (b) *nontechnical materials alone* (books, programmed print materials, syllabi, assignment sheets), or (c) *human beings* — instructors and/or students, alone or in appropriate combinations with other persons, instruments, or media. Such analysis of functions should provide clues as to ways of insuring "best fit" between human and nonhuman resources available to the program. It should also emphasize what should be a fairly obvious fact: that some, but certainly not all, learning experiences require human (instructor) intervention.

This consideration of the nonhuman resources of the institution will not be complete without attention to a number of other essentials. The institutional, school or college, and departmental budgets must be considered. Are more or fewer funds justified for the particular system or sub-system, for example? Are physical facilities — classrooms, "wet" and "dry" study carrels, large-group installations, small-group discussion rooms, and the like — suitable and available? If not, will it be possible to provide them — and over what period of time? Are the institution's administrative policies and regulations (including the "academic") in tune with the system? Will class attendance rules, for example, block intentions to facilitate flexibility in use of student time? Are there *places* for students to study if they are not in classrooms?

The fifth stage of the system process involves its implementation and the proper management of several important logistical matters. Again, decisions at this level will be made in relation to the "realities" of instructional objectives. The first question must be: Which learning experiences (which student activities) will contribute best to the achievement of those objectives? But even this question must be hedged by several other questions which come closer to specifics: Which must be offered through "human" mediation? Which need not be? Which must be offered in large-group, which in small- or medium-group, which in independent study formats? Which is to be visualized? Which is to be "one-way"? Which is to be "participative" — with the give-and-take of oral analysis and discussion? In what sequence and with what redundancy should they be? Finally, how may the answers to all these questions be used to formulate an orchestrated, workable instructional program?

The final stage of the systems approach described here involves program evaluation and improvement. Original planning will already have given attention to intended *outcomes* and to the kinds of measures and data that will indicate when those outcomes have been reached. Changes in students between the beginning and ending of instruction will be of prime importance: What do they now know (facts, principles) that they did not know before? What skills have they developed (or improved) in using their new knowledge or in approaching the study and investigation of problems in the field of instruction? How do they *feel* about the subject — in its relation to a future job, as an area of civic concern, as a future field of academic specialization? Means must be developed and refined to measure these changes; judgments must be made concerning the value or implications of changes they discern.

Evaluations must also be made for all other important parts of the system: How effective was the professorial staff? The course materials — text, syllabus, handout? Each important learning experience or assignment? The physical facilities? The media and media services supplied for individual study or large- or small-group instruction? How functional and how valid are the measures of change resulting from the program?

Finally, of course, the measures and evaluations must be studied in an effort to discover aspects of the system which will need improvement the next time around.

Assuming the foregoing brief description of the so-called "systems approach" to college and university instruction to be a fairly accurate indicator of promising forefront trends, what are some of its more general implications for media? In my opinion, the following are significant:

College and university librarians must begin to give more than lip service to the desirability of providing, on their campuses, a full range of communication services required in the modern curriculum.

They must appreciate and be guided in their actions by the fact that it is not enough for libraries simply to provide *access* to information in these various forms. Rather they must be concerned about how such information is *used* in efforts to achieve some end. Thus they must themselves understand and be skillful, and be able to help others understand and be skillful, in using various communication media, processes, and techniques.

College and university librarians — as "media" professionals — must view their resources from the point of view of the questions:

—What is to be communicated (the content, the "message")?
—To whom?
—For what purposes (objectives)?
—Through what media (or channels)?
—Under what circumstances or conditions (environment, locations, employing which procedures)?
—With what results (effects, changes in behavior)?

Media and media services must be regarded as *integral* to the teaching-learning process, not simply as peripheral extras which may be dispensed with when short of funds or time. The college or university librarian has the right to expect (or at least must have the license to seek) the commitment of instructional administration to this concept. This commitment will be expressed by at least four elements: (1) financial support and recognition and suitable reward of faculty participation in efforts to improve instruction through innovative uses of new media, (2) adequate capital investment in necessary space, facilities, equipment, and materials, (3) sufficient qualified professional and technical staff to assist instructors in finding or developing materials and in using scheduling, and maintaining technical equipment required, and (4) a faculty vitally interested in improving the quality of teaching and learning.

Foremost among the further requirements for satisfactory implementation of the systems approach to college instruction which has been described here are the following:

More creative (as opposed simply to adaptive) applications of technology to teaching-learning problems.

Consideration, perhaps first, to the special requirements and mediation opportunities presented by large-enrollment core courses in the institution's curriculum. Along with this, more attention to the creation (locally, if necessary; cooperatively with other institutions, or even commercially, if feasible) of tightly-planned, validated multimedia "packages" designed especially for such courses and fully capable of being enriched, edited, or otherwise altered, as necessary, to meet unique local requirements.

Essentially, what has been said here adds up to this: College and university librarians must act on an understanding of the fact that their functions are changing. Libraries must now be multipurpose; librarians must be concerned with how information is found, manipulated, assessed, and used to achieve instructional purposes. Libraries are not simply repositories of inert data waiting to be called to service. They must be active, essential cogs in a changing, emerging instructional system. It seems obvious that they have never achieved their full potential. Perhaps their moment has now arrived.

CHANGING LIBRARY AND INFORMATION SERVICE TECHNIQUES AND TECHNOLOGY

Allen Kent

Professor Kent is director of the University of Pittsburgh's Office of Communications Services. Mr. Kent, a graduate of City College of New York, has held positions with the Massachusetts Institute of Technology, the Battelle Memorial Institute, and the Center for Documentation and Communication Research at Case Western Reserve University. He came to the University of Pittsburgh in 1963 to establish and direct its Knowledge Availability Systems Center and to serve as professor in the Graduate School of Library and Information Sciences.

Professor Kent's main professional interests concern information storage and retrieval, and documentation and library science. He has written more than one hundred papers for professional journals, and has authored or edited (in some instances, as a co-author or co-editor) eighteen books. He has organized and conducted numerous national and international conferences on documentation and information retrieval. Mr. Kent is a member of many professional organizations among which are the American Institute of Chemists, the American Association for the Advancement of Science, the American Chemical Society, the American Society for Information Science, and the Special Libraries Association. He is also a member of the Advisory Committee, ERIC Clearinghouse on Early Childhood Education, and chairman of the National Advisory Committee on Information Systems of the National Institute of Neurological Diseases and Blindness. Professor Kent was appointed to his present position at the University of Pittsburgh in January 1970.

CHANGING LIBRARY
AND INFORMATION SERVICE
TECHNIQUES AND TECHNOLOGY

Change in library and information service is in the eyes of the beholder. It is either evolutionary or revolutionary, trivial or meaningful, existent or nonexistent, all depending upon: which part of the system is being observed; whether observed from the point of view of system designer or operator; or whether observed from the point of view of the user.

For example, if one were to borrow a book today from the Hillman Library at the University of Pittsburgh, one would find, to a high probability, a folded punched card in the book pocket, which would be used — together with a punched identification card (issued to faculty, students, and others associated with the University) — to record the transaction of:

(1) borrowing a given book,
(2) loaned on a given date,
(3) due back on another,

so that a computer could dun the borrower if the book were not returned at the appropriate time.

This might well be the user's only contact with the computer-based circulation system in the library. What would not be visible would be the quiet revolution taking place behind the scenes to automate the business of running the library. But most of these matters are not exciting to people today since what is being done is similar to what modern business is doing in making more efficient the handling of information regarding purchasing, budgeting, stock and inventory control, materials handling, billing, and like processes.

If one were to consult the card catalog of the library, a printed card would be viewed which may have been purchased from the Library of Congress to obviate the need of having many libraries catalog the same book — imperfectly (from a user's point of view) — when the Library of Congress imperfect cataloging may be purchased at less expense.

There is a quiet revolution taking place here, too, with the Library of Congress beginning to make this information available on magnetic tapes so that catalog input and output functions may be automated eventually. One may even be able to consult the catalog on a video tube, making it possible to identify a wanted book without manipulating cards or card trays, but using instead a vertical and horizontal "joy stick."

There is even a library overseas that has installed a bibliophone which permits the call number of a book to be dialed and leads to the closing of appropriate relays, the activation of a signal light and buzzer in the appropriate section of the stacks, and the alerting of a page to pull the desired book from the shelf. The page places it on a gravity conveyer system and the book is delivered "automatically."

There is considerable evidence of increasing use of microforms — unit record microfiche — particularly in the government document area, from which disposable replicas or full-size blowbacks may be obtained conveniently and inexpensively.

In addition, the ever-present page copier has made longhand plagiarism and other copyright violations economical and convenient.

Then there is the TWX substitute for the telephone and the postal system in interlibrary loan which can speed up the sharing of resources among libraries.

But none of these changes, regardless of how viewed by the beholder, will be as meaningful as the one that relates to the entry of the library into the field of computer-based information retrieval, or more accurately, the entry of computer-based information retrieval into the library.

Suppose you were to approach the card catalog — or the reference librarian — with a desire to retrieve a book whose author and title you have forgotten — but you remember that it is a *small book* with a *red cover* and that the protagonist promised to *marry her* in the *sixth chapter*. Most would agree that a search based on these criteria would be unproductive — because the cataloging would not have elucidated the subjects (or analytics) of concern in this search. One might say that these are not "proper" analytics, but it would be turning one's back to the most important problem, generically, which faces people who consult libraries — that is, to find material based on precise but idiosyncratic points of view that were not considered "proper" or generally useful analytics during the cataloging process.

It is the problem faced by an engineer, for example, who wishes to locate references to construction materials that have a number of desirable properties in common, which properties he can recite with precision. But he does not know the name of the material — which is often the very analytic that is used as the primary index entry. There are increasing numbers of such requirements so that it may be necessary to suggest that library and information *service* should involve a new concept of service — that is, meeting the needs of others (those who *use* rather than design or operate systems). This concept may be articulated as:

Satisfying the need for access to recorded knowledge by providing rapidly, conveniently, economically, and with precision, that portion of the current or previous literature that will be useful
—to a particular individual,
—at a particular time,
—for a particular problem or interest,
—and in a form that is useful to him,
regardless of
—where it was generated,
—in what form or language,
—or how it must be located or processed.

The utopian dream is to have information available on the day of publication, neatly translated into one's mother tongue, and packaged in quanta which are of infinitely variable size and content. If the above is accepted as a goal of library and information service, then the changing techniques and technology can be viewed in relation to the fundamental goal.

A number of factors have stimulated change:

(1) The time scale of information gathering for decision-making and control has been reduced drastically. This change corresponds to increases in the rates with which competitive activity, international aggressive action, and changes in public

opinion can deteriorate economic, military, and political situations.

The increasing internationalism of industrial, educational, and political organizations has been leading to increasing emphasis on information for decision-making and control derived from many sources and geographic areas not formerly considered important. This trend has increased the need for obtaining and providing information quickly which heretofore could be transmitted on a more leisurely basis.

(2) The increasing complexity of the problems of society has led to a consequent requirement for information from an ever-widening diversity of fields. This has resulted in the need to achieve insight into otherwise obscure or uncertain situations through the processing of large amounts of fragmentary information from widely scattered subject fields.

(3) There has been a dramatic increase in the amount of information that is freely available (i.e., published in one form or another), resulting in the characterization of the situation as an information explosion or avalanche. This situation has three dimensions of frustration:

   (a) The impossibility of an individual reading and remembering all of the literature that has a reasonable probability of being of later use.

   (b) The economic impossibility of individuals or their organizations processing for later retrieval the majority of literature of probable pertinent interest.

   (c) The breakdown of traditional library tools (e.g., the card catalog) in coping effectively with the detailed requirements of individuals in identifying information pertinent to a given problem.

(4) Various agencies aside from the library have undertaken information processing and disseminating functions. These include governmental agencies, professional and trade associations, universities, and profit-making industries. This trend has led to an unquantifiable overlap in processing and services.

Change in library and information service has also been stimulated by the availability of new tools, new means of information organization, and new means of dissemination.

and periodical literature in its classical form is becoming less and less convenient as the scope of interest of scholars becomes increasingly interdisciplinary and the quantity of literature of potential relevance becomes greater.

Communication among scholars through personal contacts, although increasing dramatically, is not likely to provide assurance that even the most fruitful contacts can be assured in a timely way through serendipitous discovery of communities of interests.

An impressive array of centralized and specialized information services, both discipline- and mission-oriented, is available, under development, or being planned. It has been hypothesized that these services will be augmenting or, in some cases, replacing the traditional library services that have been used by scholars in many or even most fields of endeavor. But exploitation of each of these new services, many computer-based, involves overt expenditures of funds which exceed the budgets for purchase of books and other materials of the library system. These overt expenditures, when multiplied by the number of services that are now and may soon be available, present a budget dilemma that has not previously been contemplated seriously by the university administration.

It is not enough to say that funds are not available to support these new services that are now or will be demanded by the scholarly community. Rather, like the conclusion reached in contemplating increasing budgets for conventional libraries (that some academic programs cannot be maintained without ready access to adequate library collections), so it may be said for these new services that some programs should be excluded from the curriculum if ready access to these new services cannot likewise be assured.

We, therefore, start from the premise that the faculty and students are to be provided with the most effective secondary information services that may be technologically feasible. It is known, however, that the university will never be able to create such services *de nova* and that it would always be necessary to interrelate, on some basis or other, with many centralized discipline- or mission-oriented services. This relationship would involve acquisition of, or remote access to, search-ready files, mostly involving the use of computers for exploitation purposes.

It is assumed that the costs of providing such service at the level and frequency desired will eventually exceed the ability of the university to cover such costs when the expected lease, royalty, capital, and operating expenses are all taken into account. Accordingly, a basis for amortizing basic operating costs over a group of users larger than the university itself must be sought.

Thus, successive expansion of the base of users must be considered, starting from the university group, to:

(1) other universities in the region,

(2) other nonprofit organizations,

(3) industrial organizations.

But from experience gained in attempting to serve a wide spectrum of nonuniversity users in the region through a single data base, it becomes obvious that many, if not most, organizations are not willing to pay the full costs of obtaining searching services unless a "one-stop" service is offered. That is, assurance is demanded that the search results are based on exploitation of all of the data bases relevant to a given interest.

It is entirely reasonable for fee-paying users of information services to demand such assurance, since otherwise other sources would have to be exploited by the users independently, with attendant substantial fees, but without obviating uncertainty as to the extent of overlap in coverage among the services exploited.

This situation provides an additional incentive to the university to interrelate with as many services as are willing and able to provide access to their data bases for purposes of local or regional exploitation.

In this circumstance, programs must be planned which would:

(1) Identify departments, schools, and centers at the university which have an interest in devoting senior professional time to the evaluation of available data bases in their areas of subject expertise.

(2) Determine the means and conditions under which the holders of the data bases would provide access to their services, either on a decentralized or remote basis.

(3) Estimate the costs involved in offering services from available data bases.

The next step is to consider alternative operational modes for offering services from these data bases:

(1) vertically and essentially independent,

(2) horizontally, that is, taking advantage of common unit functions, facilities, and equipment.

Alternative organizational modes must be contemplated, involving:

(1) total integration with the library system,
(2) establishment of a computer-based information center co-ordination unit.

It is expected that a formal, campus-based information system must be established in order to provide operational services to faculty and students. It is hypothesized that such operational services would necessarily involve an annual budget commitment by a university which could be maintained without substantial income from outside the walls of the university. Accordingly, a cost recovery unit must be organized, which must introduce the services to individuals and organizations in the area.

But it is not easy to exact user fees of the size and quantity that will recover costs. One of the reasons for this can be traced back to the Andrew Carnegie library programs which established an attitude that access to recorded information should be democratized—the mechanism being the free public library. Once the Andrew Carnegie money was used up it was expected that the community would use public moneys to keep the library going.

In today's environment, the Federal government is acting in an analogous manner with regard to information services. Seed money is being provided to a few institutions to do the necessary research and development which would democratize access to recorded information, with the objective that useful services would soon be paid for by the community of users.

Today, the community of users needed to attain critical mass (i.e., to amortize cost of service) is sufficiently numerous that they must be drawn from a region, rather than from a single institution. In order to gather such a large group of users who are willing to pay the requisite fees for service, a marketing activity is needed.

This marketing activity involves advertising, direct mail, and personal visits, the cost of which must be figured into service fees, making them substantially higher than may seem obvious when considering raw processing costs alone.

This cost recovery unit has a difficult marketing problem. It relates to the style of "selling" that is needed in order to attract fee-paying customers and to keep them.

The university has selling expertise of a different kind — the long-range, big-ticket "soft sell" — to attract endowment and foundation grants. In this type of selling, no hard guarantees are made that a specific product will emerge; rather, the only promise made is that the best effort of qualified faculty will be devoted to the problem in hand.

This type of selling will not attract fee-paying customers to an information center, university-based or not. The "hard sell," the guarantee of a quality product, and real attention to scheduled delivery dates, are the requirements. The traditional faculty member is not the type of person needed to do this. Rather, the tough, hard-hitting, lapel-grabbing type who has been seasoned in industrial competition is a "must." This type clashes with the traditions of a faculty. But, if the public service responsibility of a university is to be taken seriously, then the realities of the marketplace must be taken seriously as well.

What are the rewards for this type of person? A challenging assignment — certainly! But the normal rewards of tenure are not available to this type of person, and so higher salary standards must be established to overcome this limitation. Of course, the ultimate reward is security — the individual having acquired a special competence that permits mobility at will.

And this type of security is critical, since the final prize that the university may be awarded for success (i.e., creation of a profitable enterprise) is the requirement to divest itself of the activity.

What a lot of trouble this is for a university and especially a library! It may cause one to wonder whether it is all worth the candle. Why is there observed a need for changing library and information service? Is it the technology and techniques that created the demand for change, or was there a firm demand that led to the development of new techniques and technology?

It was neither, really. If we look at the four relevant technologies:

(a) logical capabilities of computers,
(b) "conversational" capabilities of time-sharing computers,
(c) data, voice, and image communication,
(d) condensed image storage,

we note that each was developed for purposes other than library and information service, and yet applied at the appropriate time.

(a) *The logical capabilities of computers.*

Let us go back to the requirement for a *small book* (*author* and *title* unknown) which has a *red cover* and in which the protagonist promised to *marry her* in the *sixth chapter*. A reference question which specifies that all of these "analytics" are available, when translated into computer, boolean algebra, suggests a logical product strategy which may be conducted economically by computer — if the appropriate analytics have been identified during initial analysis.

(b) *"Conversational" capabilities of time-sharing computers.*
The reference "dialog," when it takes place in a traditional library, involves the "negotiation" of a question between the user and the librarian in an attempt to rationalize differences between the idiosyncrasies of the user's interest and the "normal," generic analytics provided by catalogers in their processing of library materials.

The intervention of computers in the search process does not obviate the need for a "dialog" — permitted in time-sharing computer facilities through conversational, interactive programs.

(c) *Data, voice, and image communication.*
The hypothesis of the resource-sharing information network is that appropriate linkages will be available which would permit effective communication between the user and many information resources, so that the organization of files may be learned (perhaps by computer-assisted instructional routines) through data linkages. Voice linkages would provide reinforcement by contact with expert knowledge, either in subject matter or file organization, or both. Image transmission linkages would permit the viewing of materials identified from a remote file in order to ascertain relevance, before the commitment may be made to transmit large quantities of images at considerable expense.

(d) *Condensed image storage.*
If image transmission costs are not within reason it is possible to contemplate the maintenance of comprehensive libraries in microform, at low image unit cost, in many locations, so that local reference would be feasible.

These four technologies represent the rationale for information networks, and it would not be too hard, given these four available technologies, to speculate in terms of the library and information service of the future:

All arriving and all existing data . . . are photographed at a considerably reduced scale on film. Instead of large runs,

only several copies of such microfilm are produced and are
sent to me or several information centers. These centers
transmit continuously . . . all the data available in them at
a tremendous sequence frequency of frames of microfilm,
reaching, for example, a million per second. With such a
transmission speed all data accumulated by humanity can be
transmitted . . . within a comparatively brief time interval
. . . something like several minutes.

Any frame of the microfilm can be received in any place
on a special television screen equipped with a selecting de-
vice. All the instructions, classification schemes, tables of
contents of the microfilm with indication of the number of
frames, and code designation required for the use of such a
televiser are transmitted at the start of the microfilm, thereby
eliminating the need for using any kind of printed
information.

. . . It is difficult to overestimate the flexibility and effectiveness of such an imaginary method of storing and disseminating data. Undoubtedly such a method or something analogous
to it will turn out to be cheaper than the existing methods,
when the volume of data will reach definite limit.

. . . In spite of the fact that the information service of the
future described above is quite fantastic, all the technical
units required for its realization are in existence at the present
time and being constantly improved.

This speculation was conducted by V. P. Cherenin in a paper
published almost fifteen years ago and translated into English fourteen
years ago. Today, only parts of the speculation are translated into
reality — but only with regard to library operations and not for user
service — although the technology is fully here, as it was some fifteen
years ago.